# Stoning Demons

An Informed Patient's Perspective on Complex PTSD and Marijuana-Supported Therapy

## Book 3, Physical Health and Complex PTSD

*****

By Kimberly Callis

PRINT EDITION

Copyright © 2014 Kimberly Callis

ISBN 978 15 0303 2644

*****

This eBook is licensed for your personal use only. This eBook may not be re-sold or given away to other people. If you would like to share this book with another person, please purchase an additional copy for each recipient. If you are reading this book and did not purchase it, or it was not purchased for your use only, then please return to Smashwords.com and purchase your own copy.

Thank you for respecting the hard work of this author.

# Physical Health and CPTSD

*"There are wounds that never show on the body that are deeper and more hurtful than anything that bleeds."*

Laurell K. Hamilton

I want to challenge you to think about post-traumatic stress disorders in a new way... to move beyond thinking of PTSD as mental illness and see it for the systemic neuroendocrine disorder that disrupts the normal balance of energy, emotion and functioning.

Most of the more common symptoms of PTSD – anxiety, depression, confusion, eating disorders, addiction and even suicidality – can also have physiological sources. In the majority of cases, there are underlying illnesses and chronic imbalances that contribute to mental and emotional symptoms.

I had to learn this myself after I was diagnosed with Complex PTSD several years ago; a disorder stemming from childhood trauma that affects development and is compounded by recurrent traumatic experiences and chronic stress into adulthood.

While the experience of specific types of trauma and stress can affect a person's psychology in different ways, recurring traumas and chronic stress, in general, have a pervasive and particularly damaging effect on physical health.

The pathways are similar in nearly all cases; chronic activation or over-stimulation of the stress response. This response is also known as fight-or-flight.

Biologically, all emotions are supported by chemistry. All thoughts are supported by neurobiology. This is the chemistry and electricity of who we are and how we experience our lives. Being unwell mentally – especially when symptoms are chronic – generally means there is some corresponding imbalance in the body, one or more comorbid chronic conditions that influence cognition, emotions and mood. Just look at how stress affects the body and the mind.

> **Lasting recovery from Complex PTSD means focusing on more than just psychology**

Chronic health issues can reinforce and complicate psychological symptoms in a feedback loop that makes the sufferer feel as if they will never truly recover. That's how I felt, at least... until I started looking more deeply into my condition.

The way I discovered the relationship of physical and mental health for myself was difficult and involved. I researched and read as many medical and scientific papers as I could after my diagnosis. I took courses on psychology and biology online. I was a bit obsessed with understanding what was going on with me.

I wasn't happy to think that suddenly everything had gone wrong in my mind... it seemed like it was more than just something in my head.

In line with the commonly accepted definition of Complex PTSD, I had an extended list of symptoms beyond the American Psychiatric Association's Diagnostic and Statistical Manual classifications for PTSD and included all of the markers for Disorders of Extreme Stress as well.  This was the legacy of neglect and abuse I experienced as a child, but it wasn't just in my head... it was bound in my body.

I was only in my early forties, but my physical health was failing fast. I had a number of illnesses that had been affecting my health for years.  It seemed like every other word in my medical file was "chronic".  I was in bad shape and it was all linked in some way to chronic nervous system and endocrine system issues... all tied to a cycle of stress that had started more than 40 years before.

### Journal Excerpt: Stillness

> *Sometimes I am amazed at how still my body can be. There is a place I can go to, deep inside myself, where I just don't feel what my body is doing. It's quiet and still...dark and warm. Sometimes it's a peaceful place to be. Sometimes it's frightening... a confrontation with my demons.*
>
> *I let myself go to this place so much that my body simply wasted away. I built the softest walls around me... those that give others support and comfort. I mothered and cared for others while I starved myself of the things I needed most. Something in me was broken.*
>
> *It wasn't just the pain in my body telling me that I was beyond repair... it was the voices in my head telling me I was beyond hope and not worth fixing. I was convinced that my demons were within me as justice for my weakness of character and mind. I was certain that there was nothing in front of me, except the blackness that had taken everything that was ever good in my father. I suppose I had finally lived up to his prediction of me. I was stupid and worthless.*

*My mistakes of the last several years haunted me in those black times when my body was shut down for healing. I banished myself to a crappy little apartment and a room the size of the smallest walk-in closet I had during my prosperous years. The army cot and Ikea mattress I slept on reinforced the pain in my wretched little body and rang out a karmic lesson I was sure I deserved.*

*My only sunlight were the days that I felt well enough in mind and body to drag myself to the office. There were times that reminded me of home and teams that came together for a shared task and finished as friends. I found that again. Here, in a country I had learned to detest among people I thought as cold as the Dutch winters. These friends helped me rediscover a love for people. It restored a faith I questioned as a ridiculous fairy tale, even though I kept my friends at a distance.*

*I had no trouble with openness. I discovered that losing my battle with myself meant that I had lost a connection with my ego. There was just no point in avoiding truths, especially fundamental ones. Somewhere the gentle support of friendship helped me face those demons in my darkest days, my weakness of spirit had convinced me that mortality would soon show itself, my openness allowed me to face answers to questions that I had forgotten I asked.*

*I slowly found myself in this dark place, and I was small.*

*When the 'episodes' started I wasn't ready. They hit me hard. I had burned what little energy I had left in my body in those brief weeks of living well. I tried to keep up with obligations I had made when I could keep a heavy schedule. I was down to 41.5kgs ( 91 lbs ) within three weeks.*

*I rediscovered the feeling of being afraid. I was afraid of not having life. I was afraid of not having the tomorrow I could make for myself. In this I had found a horizon, somehow there really was a tomorrow. It was a lifeline of sorts. It made me reach out for help when my body started shutting down on me. It made me place the need of my body above the torment of my mind. It made me face life and choose for it.*

*It was the strangest battle. I thought that I could just get in there with the doctors again and get my body back. I could foresee a familiar path with doctors, scans, surgeries and recoveries. I could see a time when I would be back in action, my old self. I had a long look at where I was and I was in shocking condition. Whatever was ahead of me on this familiar road was not going to happen easily to a body in this poor state. I needed to get a handle on things.*

*First, we [the doctors and I] needed to figure out what we were up against. I was used to medicine in the US and Australia. The system in the Netherlands was completely incomprehensible and not just because of language.*

*There were critical things missing that left me feeling sometimes abandoned, sometimes ridiculously unworthy and unimportant, and sometimes completely adrift in a lack of information. I needed to know what was going on inside me. There was just no urgency and there was little clarity in conversations with my doctors. I missed the comfort of the care I had in Australia, with the team of doctors who worked together and helped me understand how to care for myself. I had none of that here.*

*I tried to fill in the blanks for myself and failed miserably. I could find only the worst problems to associate with my condition in my research. I scared the life out of myself. The truth revealed itself in deep-set, complex problems in my abdomen and pelvis that would need to be managed for the rest of my life. I'm 40. Going on averages, the rest of my life should be a very long time.*

*When I received the results of every test, the answer from my doctors was always, 'This is permanent. You have pain medication, what more do you want?" I took this like a knife through the chest every time I heard it. I am trying to understand the nuances of the translation here. I am actually being asked what I want.*

*What a question. With all the factors of my life, this is quite a question.*

At the time that I wrote this, I didn't understand that I was suffering from Complex PTSD. I was in full self-harm mode and was starving myself to death. I remember feeling suicidal, but feeling powerless to go through with it because of the people around me.

I didn't make the connection between my failing physical health and my mental illness for quite some time. Through several years of reading and research, I developed a greater understanding of what was really going on with me. It wasn't until 2013 that I started to get a clear picture of what I needed to stop my deterioration and work toward recovering my life. I discovered a progression in symptoms related to my mental health, as well as a pattern in my experience of triggers, relapses, recovery and remission.

At some point, everything seemed to make sense. I was having so many issues because nearly every system in my body was ill, over-stressed and under-nourished. I had blood sugar regulation problems, failing eyesight, digestive issues, tremors, trembling, chronic cravings, heavy self-medication, and other health issues... which are often seen in those with have Complex PTSD. Finding that there were so many others who had a similar profile – PTSD and chronic illness – was confronting and comforting at the same time.

What I learned about the relationship of physical and mental health helped me to finally achieve a lasting remission and regain my quality of life after years of disability and loss.

The more I read, the more information I found that supported a direct and tangible relationship to physical health in PTSD studies. These facts didn't come up in my therapy and weren't presented by my doctors.

I had to discover them on my own, researching and studying until the mechanisms of stress biology became clearer to me and I had a better understanding of functional anatomy.

I began to see why childhood trauma contributed to long-term illness. I could understand how repetitive traumas and chronic stress eroded the health of key systems until both physical and mental illness set in and became debilitating. I could see the link between so many seemingly unrelated conditions and my emotional stability… and I could see why my behaviors were contributing to my poor health and eroding my wellbeing.

## Trauma Effects

As I read anything and everything I could find, I kept landing on studies that were showing a close relationship between exposure to abuse during childhood and several of the leading causes of death in adults. This made perfect sense to me! I was suffering from a list of chronic health problems. When my physical health was poor, so was my mental health. I believed there was a relationship and the connection became clearer all the time. In fact, science and medicine are focusing on this relationship, especially over the last few years.

Many studies suggest that the impact of adverse childhood experiences on adult health is cumulative. When secondary traumas occur, the risk of developing the hallmark symptoms of CPTSD – anxiety, intrusive thoughts and depression –worsen. Chronic stress can cause symptoms to increase over time as the person's physical health deteriorates.

# Chronic Health Issues

Studies have increasingly linked heart disease, cancer, lung disease, liver disease and other systemic illnesses to mental illness and connecting deeper mental illness to childhood trauma.

Looking at the many studies available on traumatic stress, results suggest that the cumulative effect of multiple traumas is a primary contributing factor in chronic illness. This is due to the degenerative effects of over-activation of the sympathetic nervous system, dysregulation in the parasympathetic nervous system, and neuroendocrine imbalance.

There is an important feedback cycle involved in physical symptoms of post-traumatic illness, coping behaviors and emotional symptoms.

Some traumas can have a fairly direct correlation to specific conditions, especially abuse resulting in injury. For example, traumatic brain injury from concussion is shown to cause neurological problems in later life. Also, childhood sexual abuse in girls has been linked to increased incidence of endometriosis, infertility and sexual dysfunction, showing the potential for damaging effects from early sexualization. Eating disorders and poor nutrition can lead to digestive and endocrine problems later in life.

When I had finished my psychotherapy and ran out of questions about my traumas, I found that CPTSD was still having an effect on my life. I still struggled with fatigue. My heart rate was often erratic. That familiar feeling of butterflies in my stomach that had always been the signal of a looming panic attack was constant... even when I had experienced no triggers or had any real stress in my life.

I felt like I was in a state of constant anxiety, but had absolutely no reason (that I was aware of) to feel the way I did.

As I started to understand more, I inventoried my symptoms, my triggers, my diet and my thoughts. But working through the psychology behind what I was suffering wasn't enough to make my anxiety or depression go away. It wasn't enough to stop the panic attacks or help me deal with stress. I did eventually found healing for my traumas, and I ran out of questions to be answered about my past. I was better, but I still wasn't well. I found symptoms arose even when I was not under emotional stress, when no triggers were present and there was no reason for me to feel what I was feeling.

I had other health issues, so I explored my medical trauma and came to terms with that, psychologically speaking. I have a history of serious illness; the worst of all is endometriosis. I also had chronic digestive system issues, a heart condition and hypoglycemia... all seemingly unrelated to my psychological condition. Or so I thought. The only connection I made was the logical fact that my mental condition seemed to get worse every time I had to deal with medical issues, especially after my most critical battle saw me in hospital for months, part of that spent in intensive care recovering from major surgery and septic infection. I understood that the situation was traumatic; I just didn't realize how great an influence it would have on me.

In fact, the co-morbidity of chronic illness in patients with Complex PTSD is remarkable. People with CPTSD commonly suffer from one or more chronic physical conditions as well, making treatment and recovery much more challenging.

The need for a holistic approach that addresses physical, emotional and mental health restoration is vital. Without a comprehensive plan, wellness is nearly impossible to achieve.

During my research, I gathered information from several studies to help me compile statistics on the correlation between Complex PTSD and chronic illness.

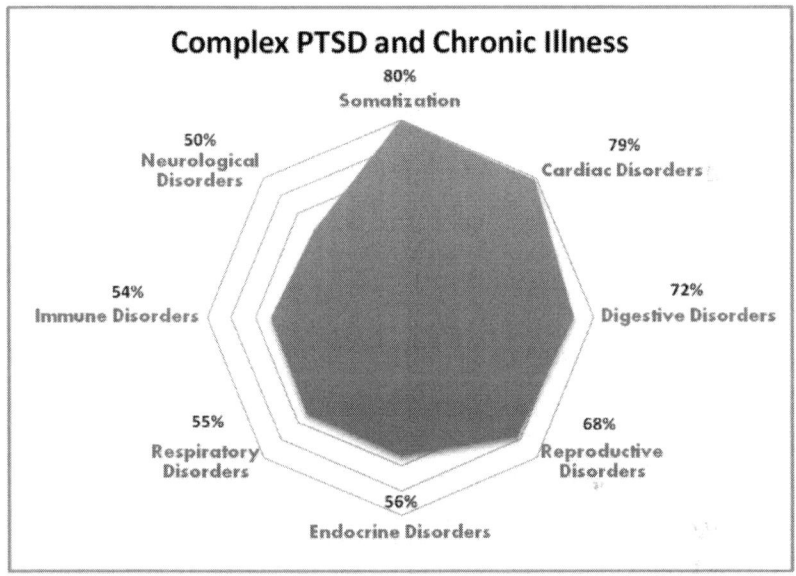

It took me years to put all the pieces together for myself. It has taken years to change my attitude and really get myself on track with the whole program, too. Focusing on my physical health had to become an ingrained behavior. Eating healthy whole foods, finding plenty of restful moments, and keeping up my exercise all have a new importance in my life.

## Somatization and Comorbid Illness

Studies show a clear relationship between early experiences of abuse, neglect and trauma with somatic diseases (e.g. high blood pressure, coronary heart disease, diabetes) in adulthood. Furthermore, there is increasing evidence that PTSD is not only associated with a higher vulnerability for comorbid mental disorders but also with an increased incidence of (psycho-) somatic disorders.

*DSM Criteria*

- *Somatization*
- *Digestive System*
- *Chronic Pain*
- *Cardiopulmonary Symptoms*
- *Conversion Symptoms*
- *Sexual Symptoms*

Biologically, somatization is related to functions of the somatic nervous system, a part of the peripheral nervous system involved in voluntary movement and the communication of sensory information like touch and pain, as well as the autonomic nervous system, which comprised of the sympathetic and parasympathetic nervous systems. Dysregulation, dysfunction, over- or under-activation of these systems can lead to a range of physical symptoms that correspond with emotional or mental symptoms.

It seems almost unfair to have this classification of symptoms in the DSM, as if they stem from psychological or psychiatric problems. It is more accurate to associate all of these issues with the body systems that are fundamentally involved.

Once I pushed beyond this view of the symptoms of Complex PTSD and started looking at biology, I could actually see the source and the solution for my condition.

In my experience with pain, for example, or more specifically, my reaction to it, led me to read more about the biological systems involved in pain and pain response, specifically the components of the peripheral nervous system, the brain and central nervous system and the endocrine system. These systems not only deal with pain, the deal with fear, stress and all manner of needs, moods and behavior.

## The Brain and Central Nervous System

As a patient with CPTSD, I believe that is important to understand neurological symptoms that may present as mental illness. There are aspects of my condition that are more neurological than psychological.

I am not confident that the physiological basis was considered in my case when I was going through diagnosis and early treatment. One example is the cognitive issues I deal with even though my other CPTSD symptoms are in remission. I did not have any neurological tests as part of my diagnosis nor did I have a medical interview that focused on any neurological symptoms I had experienced. Dealing with the residual cognitive effects is frustrating, but I have found some hope that my condition will improve the longer I am in remission and have little need to medicate with cannabis.

There are four key areas of the brain which may be affected by complex post-traumatic stress disorder:

- the prefrontal cortex
- the amygdala
- the hippocampus
- the paraventricular nucleus in the hypothalamus

The link between developmental trauma, CPTSD and chronic illness is becoming clearer as research looks more openly at the connection between mental and physical health. What is becoming apparent is that the population reporting chronic systemic illnesses, especially involving the brain and nervous system and the endocrine system, have a high incidence of traumatic experiences as children.

### *Components of the Nervous System*

While the entire nervous system can be affected by trauma and chronic stress, the primary components involved in Complex PTSD symptoms and related conditions are within the peripheral nervous system.

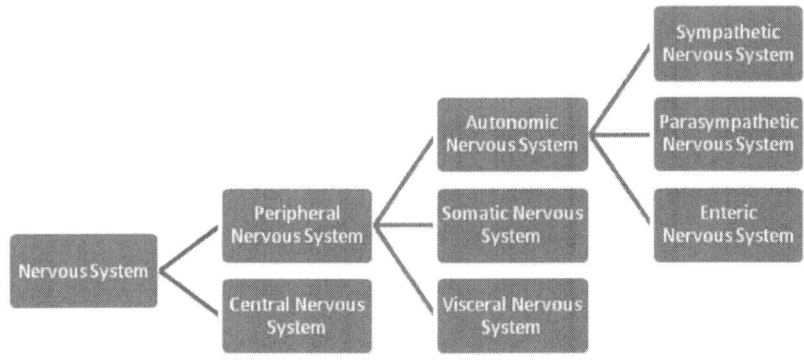

*Adapted from: Wikipedia, Nervous System*

## Peripheral Nervous System

The peripheral nervous system includes all of the nervous system components outside of the brain and central nervous system. The peripheral nervous system connects the body to the central nervous system and the brain. It is the system that communicates sensation, pain, commands for movement, reaction to stimulus, physiological processes and all autonomic functions.

The peripheral nervous system has several components, each of which carries out vital functions:

1. The somatic nervous system, which includes the nerves that connect voluntary muscle and sensory receptors to the brain

2. The autonomic nervous system, which carries information to manage arousal and rest.

The autonomic nervous system is involved in all of the common symptoms of post-traumatic disorders. Anxiety, depression, hyper-arousal and even dissociative states are physiological responses to stress. Stress can be psychological, but it can also be purely physical as well, brought on by exertion, hunger, blood sugar fluctuations, toxins, stimulants and other sources.

The autonomic nervous system is comprised of the sympathetic, parasympathetic and enteric nervous systems.

Some of the systemic conditions that are seen which involve dysfunction in the peripheral nervous system include:

- Anxiety, hyper-arousal, insomnia and cognitive difficulties
- Cardiac disease, especially arrhythmias, angina and inflammatory illness
- Fibromyalgia, chronic pain
- Tremors or trembling, minor PNS seizures
- Metabolic-related conditions
- IBS and digestive disorders

When the sympathetic nervous system is over-activated (by trauma) or chronically stimulated (by stress), its functioning can deteriorate leading to systemic health issues. This part of the nervous system, just as any other, can suffer neurological dysfunction and it can lead to significant disorders in the associated organs and glands.

*On top of this, our entire nervous system is assaulted by toxins in our food that mimic neurotransmitters, cause endocrine system disruption and flood our cells with excitory chemicals.*

Functions of the Autonomic Nervous System related to trauma and stress:

|  | Sympathetic Nervous System | Sympathetic Nervous System | Enteric Nervous System |
|---|---|---|---|
| **Senses** | • Dilates pupil | • Constricts pupil |  |
| **Brain & Cognition** | • Diverts glucose to body<br>• Isolates attention Increases alertness | • Promotes glucose supply to brain<br>• Diffuses attention<br>• Stimulates rest and sleep | • Signals hunger<br>• Stimulates cravings |
| **Cardiovascular system** | • Accelerates heart, constricts arterioles | • Inhibits heart, dilates arterioles | • |
| **Endocrine System** | • Inhibits pancreas and adrenals<br>• Stimulates release of adrenaline and cortisol | • Stimulates<br>• Stimulates uptake of serotonin and production of GABA | • Controls stomach motility and secretion |
| **Digestive System** | • Inhibits intestinal motility | • Stimulates intestinal motility | • Controls intestinal motility |

|  | Sympathetic Nervous System | Sympathetic Nervous System | Enteric Nervous System |
|---|---|---|---|
| **Reproductive System** | • Sexual arousal | • Sexual release | • |
| **Mood and Emotions** | • Controls production of adrenaline and cortisol | • Stimulates production of endo-cannabinoids | • Controls production of serotonin |

The sympathetic nervous system is the primary component of our nervous system that is involved in the fight-or-flight response. This is the control center that sends signals to the key glands and organs to speed the heart, send energy to the large muscles, stop digestion and focus the attention on survival. If this system is over-stimulated by stress, toxins or poor health on a continual basis, degradation of the system would show as chronic dysregulation in arousal, anxiety, digestion and attention. The sympathetic nervous system connects the central nervous system to key organs and glands in the body.

The parasympathetic nervous system is involved in returning everything to normal. It helps regulate rest, digestion, calmness and healing. If this system is dysregulated, there will be sleep issues presenting as insomnia or hypersomnia, excessive hunger or lack of appetite, depression and even dissociation. The swing depends on whether this system is over- or under-stimulated. Blood sugar imbalances can dramatically influence the parasympathetic nervous system. The parasympathetic nervous system is responsible for managing metabolic rate. The parasympathetic nervous system also connects the central nervous system to glands and organs.

Both the sympathetic and parasympathetic nervous systems use hormones and neurotransmitters to perform their various functions. These biochemicals connect with cell receptors specially designed to match them, triggering processes within the cell that support homeostasis. Cell processes utilize enzymes, proteins, sugars, electrolytes and other critical bioresources to perform their functions well. Imbalances – deficiencies or excessive levels – of biochemical resources can cause problems in any of these structures: organs, glands, neurons and other cells.

When imbalances are chronic, damage can result in illness. Symptoms accumulate and worsen as time goes on, especially when stress keeps the sympathetic nervous system in overload and represses healing balance of the parasympathetic nervous system.

There is another component of the autonomic nervous system that is also involved in PTSD symptoms, the enteric nervous system. This system primarily resides in the gut. In fact, most of the body's serotonin is produced in the bowels. A person experiencing serious digestive system illness may have complications with emotional balance because it can cause changes in serotonin levels.

Damage to the digestive system from eating disorders, excessive sugar, poor diet, nutrient deficiencies and chemical additives in our food and water must be resolved in order to see lasting recovery from depression.

## Endocrine System

Learning about endocrine system function (and dysfunction) has helped me tremendously in managing my CPTSD. Knowing that I am dealing with a biological process that is sensitive and that, for me, requires constant tuning through nutrition, stress management and biochemical defense helps me to shift my thoughts about my disorder. It helps me to better understand my emotions and to deal with them in constructive ways.

As mentioned earlier, the paraventricular nucleus – a part of the brain – can be affected by CPTSD. The paraventricular nucleus controls the neuroendocrine system's response to stress.

Dysfunction in this system has been also been linked with alcoholism and substance abuse, but the specific role of this part of the brain has not been fully explored. Perhaps further research will shed light on this and help shed light on the physiological relationship between chronic stress and addiction.

To understand the effects of CPTSD and how they relate to the neuroendocrine system, it is important to understand its components and purpose.

People who have a history of childhood trauma, especially abuse, show increased pituitary-adrenal and autonomic responses to stress compared with those who have no reported history of developmental trauma. This relationship is particularly strong in people with current symptoms of depression and anxiety.

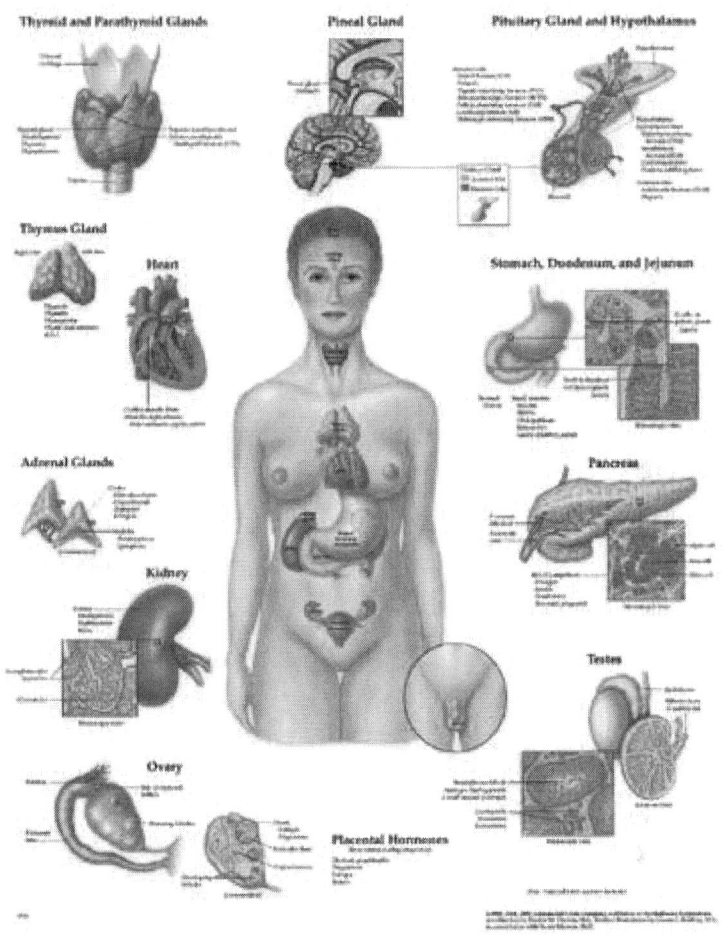

Source:
http://biologyforlunch.wikispaces.com/file/view/endo.jpg/228844036/endo.jpg

Chronic activation of the stress response can lead to endocrine dysfunction, such as adrenal fatigue, poor blood sugar regulation and metabolic dysfunction. In addition, some of the complications of CPTSD can affect the endocrine system, reinforcing symptoms and creating a feedback loop of stress activation and stress response.

When I finally confirmed my endocrine system issues, it was a revelation. Before putting it all together, I had thought I was experiencing some kind of subconscious trigger, that maybe there was something that was setting me off that I couldn't quite identify at the back of my head. I was bothered by this, especially because I really try not to be a superstitious person or someone who falls into the trap of irrationality.

Learning that there was a physical disorder underlying my feelings was liberating in a way that is hard to fully explain. I could finally stop looking for some hidden demon to explain what I was feeling. I could let go of some degree of hopelessness that came from thinking I would never be free of things that would make me feel bad. I could look for ways to naturally fix what was physically and tangibly wrong with me. I could let myself feel hopeful about being well again.

For example, I know that if I don't eat regularly and maintain my blood sugar I will feel the physical symptoms of anxiety. If I don't eat enough protein, eat too much sugar or drink too much alcohol, then I will throw off my metabolism until I can find a balance again. Fluctuations in blood sugar can lead to a release of adrenaline. Dips and spikes can result in fatigue. For someone with CPTSD, emotional swings from any source -- triggered or chemical -- are to be avoided.

Common systemic complaints with neuroendocrine dysfunction:

- Diabetes and hypoglycemia
- Electrolyte imbalance
- Anxiety and/or depression
- Adrenal fatigue

Learning about adrenal fatigue was eye-opening for me. I realized that I had been struggling with physical symptoms that were more intrusive than the thoughts and memories I was confronting with my CPTSD. Adrenal fatigue can happen when the adrenal glands function below their normal and necessary levels. This condition is generally associated with chronic stress. The primary symptom is fatigue that is not relieved by sleep – and can be mistaken for depression -- but it is not a readily identifiable with any other illness.

With adrenal stress, cortisol levels may rise and fall as the body struggles to balance. The stress response increases levels of cortisol, which can destroy healthy muscle and bone, slow down healing and normal cell replacement, hijack biochemistry needed to make hormones, impair metabolism, increase blood sugar levels, and promote storage of abdominal fat. These complications can set the right conditions for diabetes, heart disease, and suppression of the immune system. In prolonged stress, the adrenals are exhausted and cortisol remains below normal levels, which carries its own risks for long-term health.

The by-products of cortisol can depress brain activity and act as sedatives. Cortisol blocks serotonin, contributing to feelings of depression. Adrenal fatigue may also be a factor in many chronic health conditions, including:

- fibromyalgia
- hypothyroidism
- chronic fatigue syndrome
- arthritis
- menstrual difficulties

Long-term exposure to cortisol has been found to result in damage to cells in the hippocampus. This damage results in impaired learning and mood dysregulation.

Interestingly, short-term exposure to cortisol helps to create memories, called "flashbulb memories". There may be a strong relationship here to the intrusive thoughts, flashbacks and dreams that are experienced by CPTSD patients.

Cortisol can also damage other parts of the brain which control emotions, impulse control, arousal, and attention. It is easy to see why stress management for CPTSD recovery is essential. Keeping cortisol levels in check can help reduce the frequency and severity of symptoms. My experience keeps me committed to my own stress management. Whenever my stress levels are high or I've felt my fear response triggered, I know I will experience the whole range of CPTSD symptoms, sometimes for days or weeks afterward.

Sometimes sorting out the source of CPTSD episodes is therapeutic in itself. I am aware that often my symptoms are caused by some other issue besides just what I am thinking or remembering. Knowing that particular health issues, such as poor rest, poor eating habits, low blood sugar, even the physical stress of colds and flu can set off PTSD symptoms helps just as much.

## Cardiovascular System

There are many studies that provide evidence to link heart disease and psychological trauma. Elevated stress hormones, especially adrenaline and cortisol can cause spikes in blood pressure as well as abnormal heart rhythms, like tachycardia and bradycardia.

I as diagnosed with heart rhythm and structural problems in my twenties, at a time when I was really stressed and had pushed myself too hard. I had episodes of rapid, irregular heartbeat during the day and very slow heart rates during my sleep.

I was amazed to discover the association of mitral valve prolapsed in women who suffered childhood sexual abuse. Studies done over the last few decades have highlighted this relationship, providing empirical evidence and suggestions for the pathways. All of the studies highlight the association of traumatic experiences and chronic stress experienced. My case seems to be clearly reflected in these findings.

In light of this, I have become more focused on risks associated with my cardiac health. It is difficult to do all of the things that I need to do to improve my health here, but whatever health I can retain will help me reduce the cardiac symptoms that complicate my CPTSD.

Here, I can use diet and exercise to support my recovery. Improving my diet, excluding sugar and food chemicals, will help improve my heart function. My heart rate will normalize a bit and be less susceptible to biochemical fluctuations.

This can help reduce the likelihood that I will experience anxiety and panic attacks.

Exercise will improve the condition of my entire cardiovascular system, which will help improve my stress management, activate my parasympathetic nervous system, increase my energy and reduce depression. There are more benefits than I could possibly name.

Reducing life stresses and working to avoid further trauma (if possible) will help my cardiac function, limiting the activation of the sympathetic nervous system.

## Immune System

Recent findings show that people with various forms of PTSD have higher blood levels of T-cell lymphocytes and lower cortisol levels, which suggests that PTSD may increase the risk for autoimmune dysfunction. There is clinical evidence that inflammatory disorders and autoimmune diseases have their origin in chronic stress or recurrent over-activation of the sympathetic nervous system.

Chronic activation of fear and stress responses can cause severe imbalances in the immune system, especially when digestive health is compromised. The result is an increase of the body's allostatic load: the wear and tear of recurrent trauma and chronic stress.

The immune system suffers under stress. It is repressed during times of trauma and acute distress. Feedback in this cycle results in further stress and further degradation of immune function. It is a vicious cycle that directly impacts health and can lead to critical epigenetic changes, cellular death, aging and even cancer.

Strategies to improve immune function should be included in long term CPTSD recovery approaches.

## Digestive System

Damage to the digestive system from eating disorders, excessive sugar, poor diet, nutrient deficiencies and chemical additives in our food and water must be resolved in order to see lasting recovery from Complex PTSD.

I have had an eating disorder for as long as I can remember. Functioning anorexia kept me at a weight that I liked, but it took a toll on my health over the years. I would starve myself to 90 lbs and then binge until I reached 110. I repeated this cycle for decades. I only occasionally gave serious effort to fitness and nutrition. For the most part, I lived on coffee and sugar.

For years, I ignored serious illness that I knew was causing me major issues. I had debilitating pain and serious bowel constrictions with my monthly cycle and I knew it was probably endometriosis. I had seen my sister suffer from the condition. It wasn't until my early thirties that I did anything about it, even though I had my first symptoms and ongoing pain from the age of 18.

When endometriosis affected my digestive system, my complications with depression and control of my blood sugar got worse and worse. I did not understand the role of the gut in emotional health for quite a long time. Nor did I understand how low blood sugar could trigger anxiety, panic attacks and insomnia.

It wasn't until I was prescribed SSRIs that I started to be aware of what serotonin is. Even then, it took years to discover the relationship of digestive health, nutrition and emotional health. Once I got that, I was able to deal with my problems more holistically.

I stopped taking SSRIs and used nutrition and gastrointestinal wellness approaches to promote healthy serotonin levels. This meant cutting out processed foods and almost all sugar. I increased my intake of whole foods, fruits and vegetables, nuts and seeds, healthy protein and dairy. My approach involved avoiding meat on most days, but allowing myself an occasional healthy meal with meat protein.

Along with this, I added a more therapeutic approach to using marijuana. I have to maintain daily intake in order to keep up my appetite. This is fine, but I need to be cautious about not over-using and triggering sugar cravings.

Choosing to eat healthier foods that would not trigger my symptoms was beneficial in so many ways. After years of suffering from complications, I thought I would never really eat well or live without pain again.

Happily, I am nearly pain free for two years and have better digestive health than I ever remember.

## Reproductive System

My endometriosis diagnosis was a pivotal event in my life. It changed everything. I started infertility treatment, which was unsuccessful. I began a series of surgeries that would progressively remove parts of my insides, but gave me more problems and pain than I started with. A surgical mistake during one of the procedures put me in critical condition in ICU. I had a temporary stoma while I healed from the invasive exploratory surgery that found the hole burned into my intestine by a laser in a shaky hand.

This was the medical trauma that triggered my slide into PTSD.

It is hard for me to really say what came first... the endometriosis is likely a result of many things, but those things are all from the environment of my childhood.

Research has shown that early sexualization and resulting hormone imbalances are somehow related to endometriosis. The hormone imbalance is complicated by stress, but is also influenced by environmental xenohormones like estrogen-mimicking chemicals in food additives and plastics. The autoimmune classification of endometriosis means that it has systemic implications and indicates a systemic trigger.

The early sexualization is important. I believe that I would not have developed endometriosis if I was not sexually abused. I may not have developed Complex PTSD or any of the other identity, personality, psychological, psychiatric or whatever classifications I have either.... at least the parts that have such an effect on my sexuality and attachment. That early trauma directly impacted my health, to the point that recovery meant I needed to improve my physical health while doing psychotherapy in order to achieve long-term stability.

*Journal Excerpt: Ironies and Complexities...*

*Today is one of those days when the various topics I research and write about come together in personal experience. It's an endo day.*

*An endo day is one where I pretty much lay in my bed dealing with pain from my endometriosis and trying to fill my day with doing something more mental than physical. On particularly bad days, I'm usually fairly medicated and sleep most of the time. Today is not so bad. I'm only slightly medicated.*

*Sometimes my endo days are complicated by other issues... maybe I'm stressed and my anxiety is up, maybe I'm not managing my blood sugar and my moods and energy are up and down, maybe I'm dealing with triggers and my brain is steeped in rumination and fatigued with depression. All this makes the pain harder to deal with. Today is not bad at all. I'm not stressed, depressed or anxious. I'm just a little bored.*

*So, I've been digging into my research on endocrine disruptors and xenoestrogens and their relationship to endometriosis and other health issues. I'm amazed at the ironies and complexities of my life that have led me to this place.*

*1.) Early sexualization stemming from childhood sexual abuse AND exposure to endocrine-disrupting environmental toxins in childhood are both considered contributors to endometriosis.*

*2.) Early stresses (abuse and neglect) and childhood traumas (head injury from bicycle accident) contributed to development of Complex PTSD following ICU hospitalization in adulthood, a complication from endometriosis. The fact that I was trying to reconcile with my past at the time of my hospitalization is one of life's ironies, but likely contributed to the course of Complex PTSD in the years following.*

*3.) Use of leuprolide acetate (Lupron) as a treatment for endometriosis, which shuts down function of the anterior pituitary gland — a deliberate disruption to endocrine function that affects hormones. Use of this drug is also linked to increase risk of mental health issues, including depression, anxiety, psychotic symptoms and suiciality... all hallmarks of PTSD. These all set in once I started the full course of Lupron. I later realized that I had used Lupron during IVF around the time of my surgical treatments for endometriosis.*

*4.) Lupron is prescribed for other illness that are linked to exposure to environmental toxins, like prostate cancer, breast cancer, and precocious puberty. Curious. So the one thing that was prescribed for me to combat the long-term effects of toxins, contributed to the worsening of symptoms from the long-term effects of abuse? Argh.*

*I'm more committed than ever to taking a natural approach to living and healing with the hope of reducing further toxic effects on my system. In my recovery, I'm doing well on the mental health side, considering that I have come to terms with my past and found real acceptance. But, I'm still on the path to rebuilding my life, which is largely dependent now on regaining my physical health and reducing my need to medicate.*

*But, on days like this, I just have to quietly accept my limitations and find something to keep my brain happily occupied... and be happy that the symptoms are pretty mild.*

## **Endocannabinoid System**

CPTSD is not a disorder that is "in our heads"... it is a dysfunction in our bodies. Perhaps this is why marijuana plays a key role in maintaining my health. I discovered, through trial-and-error as well as research, that cannabis had a recognizable effect on my symptoms, both physical and psychological.

I became a quiet advocate for medical marijuana and spent countless hours reviewing scientific papers and articles about its value in treating Complex PTSD. When the research finally came together in a pivotal paper, *Endocannabinoid System Participates in Neuroendocrine Control of Homeostasis*, by De Laurentiis and a group of researchers from the University of Buenos Aires, I realized why marijuana had become a main component of my treatment.

According to De Laurentiis, *the endocannabinoid system has been recognized as a major neuromodulatory system, whose function is to maintain brain homeostasis.*

In my reading, I learned how the endocannabinoid system works in conjunction with the neuroendocrine system to manage homeostasis. It includes all of the functions and processes of how our bodies respond to stimuli and environment. It regulates our stress response, our use and storage of energy, production of hormones, and body temperature. Our neuroendocrine system modulates homeostasis.

I realized that marijuana wasn't just a crutch; it helped me regain control of my illness and recapture some of my health as well. The caveat was, I had to eliminate everything that could cause further neuroendocrine issues and improve my intake of healthy, healing nutrients. Along with cannabis, a healthy diet and elimination of toxins were key elements of my recovery plan.

Cannabis can help manage CPTSD symptoms and support the recovery process. Cannabis can help maintain remission, provided it is used properly and there is a deliberate approach to reducing stress and avoiding further traumatization and triggers. It is easy to get stuck using marijuana and not moving forward in recovery.

In my next book, Marijuana-Supported Therapy for Complex PTSD, I will share the recovery strategies that I found most useful. Not only will the recovery approaches for psychological recovery and growth be addressed, I will also share the vital health recovery and detoxifying methods I used to regain my balance and achieve long-term remission of my symptoms.

# Assaults on Health that Complicate CPTSD

*"If there is a single definition of healing it is to enter with mercy and awareness those pains, mental and physical, from which we have withdrawn in judgment and dismay."*

*Stephen Levine*

About one third of people with Complex PTSD do not fully recover. Many have recurrent episodes of relapse and remission. I believe that I would have been one of those people, had I not discovered all of the ways that my body was being assaulted by toxins, stress and behaviors that were keeping me from getting well.

CPTSD carries a lifelong risk for relapse, but there is quite a lot that can be done to reduce symptoms and achieve lasting periods of remission. Barring further traumas, when normal stress is reduced and there is a focus on health, remission is possible.

But, we are assaulted by agents in our normal, everyday life that can complicate symptoms. Some common toxins, including sugar, can make symptoms worse and keep a person in a constant state of physical stress.

For those with CPTSD; it may be helpful to understand more about external sources of triggers for symptoms. Many of them are hidden in foods, personal products and household chemicals that we use every day.

For me, it became quite clear that the path back to emotional health required a focus on my physical health. I had to find the right formula to reclaim my body and my mind.

I had to tackle a number of different influences on my health: diet and nutrient deficiencies, toxins, hormonal imbalance, exercise, rest and stress. This part of my recovery had to happen at the same time as my psychological therapy. I'll cover the recovery process in a later book, focusing here on the important aspects of physical health and its relationship to emotional and mental wellbeing.

## Chronic Stress

This is where my reading started, with the stress response (fear response, fight-or-flight). I thought I understood what it was and how it worked, but I really didn't know much. I had read about the relationship between signals in the body and brain that trigger creation or processing of various chemicals (hormones, neurotransmitters, sugars, proteins and electrolytes).

I learned about the relationship between these highly complex, reactive processes and stress, even the everyday kind of stress we have from living a normal first world life. I learned how traumatic response is triggered and what the cascade of reactions does to the body. I also learned that it's possible for all of these systems to become disrupted, sending off signals at the wrong time and keeping the body, mind and emotions on high alert.

But, there was nothing in the traditional approaches to treatment for any of my conditions that was going to help me make the connections I ultimately came to with personal research and a stubborn determination to learn everything I could. I suppose it's ironic that my disability gave me time to research my disability and to learn that maybe, just maybe, I never had to get to this point at all.

## Common Toxins

With a new understanding of how my body had reacted to recurrent activation of fight-or-flight, I created a symptom inventory to assist my recovery and track how I was feeling. Creating my inventory helped me as I was working on my triggers and environmental clues as well. I used it to help me find coping strategies and to help me remove unnecessary stressors in my life. I added nutrition and avoidance of toxins to my recovery plan after I learned how some stressors were actually in my food and everyday products I was using.

I learned to avoid glutamate and aspartate, neurotransmitter mimics in food that can degrade the nervous system and keep the sympathetic nervous system in overdrive. I learned about GABA and electrolyte deficiencies that were impacting my energy levels and making my head foggy. I really looked at sugar and its impact on my endocrine health and mood.

Glutamate and aspartate in various forms have increased in the processed food supply. Glutamate in its exogenous form is the most abundant neurotransmitter in the human body. It is the excitory neurochemical that alerts our bodies to "do" all the things that we do; breathe, eat, move, walk, talk, and think.

With external, artificial sources in our food supply that are close enough chemically to bind with cell receptors, we are experiencing side effects that are cumulative. The health of our nervous system is being degraded, making our peripheral nervous system more susceptible to dysfunction, over- and under-stimulation.

If you have Complex PTSD and any of the above issues, you will want to look into clean eating, complete elimination of sugar and sweeteners and chemical food additives. Incorporating better micro-nutrient management, such as management of key vitamins and minerals – especially electrolytes – is important for resetting chemical balance. Additionally, including alternative therapies like meditation, acupuncture and cannabis therapies can help support faster, longer lasting recovery.

Be prepared for it to take months or even years to feel largely recuperated. However, relief from anxiety and depression should not take more than a few weeks, if you stick to the program.

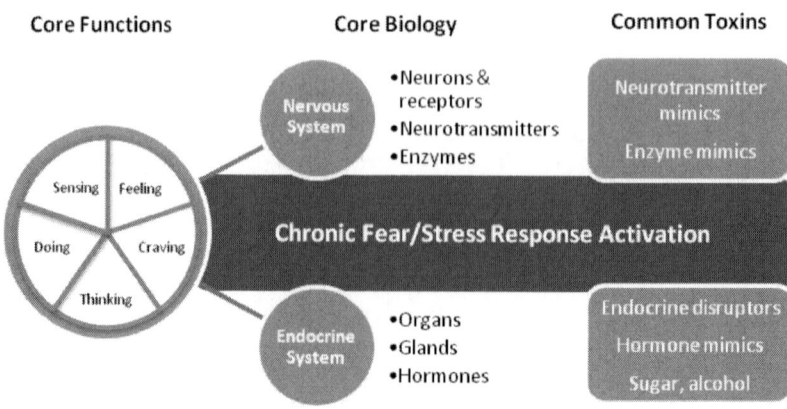

Nutritional therapies and exclusion of certain foods, food additives and chemicals is essential.

I took a simple approach to recovery, with some basic principles applied as I became better at managing my condition:

- Improving balance of nutrition toward wellness.
- Resting during depressive episodes.
- Reducing sugar and chemical food additives to alleviate anxiety.
- Allowing depression to promote rest and sleep for as long as necessary until balance is restored.
- Taking opportunities for exercise.

## Chronic Stress and Electrolyte Imbalance

One solution to relieving my CPTSD symptoms came from an unexpected place. I had been suffering from cognitive issues for years. This was one of the symptoms that I hated most because it took away my thinking brain and made it impossible for me to work. I had to give up consulting because I just couldn't thinking quickly or clearly anymore.

I didn't realize there was such a simple cause or such a handy solution.

My son did some research and came back with a grocery bag full of Powerade one day. He had found articles on cognitive issues, depression and electrolytes and wanted to see if the drinks would make any difference in how I was feeling. The effects were almost immediate.

I had the first half bottle and waited to see what would happen. Everything seemed to clear and settle. My ears stopped ringing so loudly and I was able to focus on my research. I looked into it myself.

I found what my son had seen; articles showing that imbalances in key minerals – low levels of potassium, too much sodium, poor absorption of calcium, deficiencies in magnesium – play a role in brain and nervous system function. Neurons use these biochemical resources to support cellular functions. Without the right balance, the neurons cannot function effectively.

Add to this the fact that the demand for these minerals is based on physiological processes, like stress, and again you can see why it is important to address mineral deficiencies.

Magnesium in particular is important for stress management. Adding magnesium can help address many of the symptoms common in sufferers of PTSD, including anxiety, depression, insomnia and cognitive issues.

For the last several months, I have made a point of adding key electrolytes to my diet and found relief from most of my symptoms. For the first time in years I found calm and rest... and clarity, making remission possible as long as I manage my stress levels as well.

There are many unprocessed foods that are good sources for magnesium and other minerals that are needed to support parasympathetic nervous system function.

I prefer natural food sources, rather than supplements, but I have to confess to using the quick fix of electrolyte drinks when I'm feeling bad.

# Behavioral Risks

Often, those with a history of trauma and chronic stress revert to self-soothing behaviors like addiction, binging and deprivation. Smoking, drug use, poor nutrition, toxins in foods and medication, sugar and poor sleep lead to poor health and are often linked to a history of trauma. All of these behaviors have an impact on mental wellbeing, increasing stress and complicating symptoms and resulting in poor health and lifestyle that create a downward spiral.

Discovering this gave me new motivation. I still have to keep working on my recovery, keep up with my maintenance and take other steps to protect my health... I still have to work to reclaim my nervous system and endocrine health. It's not just my body that will benefit, my mind will too.

Eating healthy whole foods, finding plenty of restful moments, and keeping up my exercise all have a new importance in my life. I've learned that sometimes just skipping a meal can cause me to have physical anxiety symptoms. Being too tired or eating too much sugar can make me feel lethargic, which feels like depression symptoms. Drinking alcohol causes blood sugar spikes and crashes which make me feel like I'm on a roller coaster of panic. Keeping a routine helps me know when I am really dealing with triggers and not imbalances in my system.

Somewhere along the line, a better method of treating my trauma and dealing with stress could have reduced the damage. At least I know now and I can work on keeping myself well and regaining my health. It's clear that I need to do certain things and manage my life carefully.

Doing it right means that I can have the healthy, balanced life I deserve. I can leave myself open to growing and enjoying what I have, instead of hiding and fearing what I have left behind me.

Finding that long term stress can cause these issues was a relief, but it also clarified what I would need for my life going forward. If I want to be well and stay well, I needed to change some of my behaviors. It reinforces my need for a low stress life – and all the decisions that drives – to support my health and long term wellness. It's helpful to know that the symptoms I typically associate with solely mental processes have a solely physical source at times. It feels that there is something within my power that I can do to make my situation better.

Given that the solution has some practicality to it, I can feel better about my future.

# How I Came to Be Here

*"For in every adult there dwells the child that was, and in every child there lies the adult that will be."*

John Connolly

There's really nothing special about my story. I'm just another one of those people who had a tough childhood. I've had some challenges in life and some successes. Life was good at times. Sometimes, I was knocked down but I picked myself up and moved on, over and over again... until I just couldn't do it anymore.

I can pinpoint the exact moment when I woke up "broken". I could no longer cope, couldn't myself together anymore. The downward spiral started from there… there was no turning back, no well of inner resilience I could tap into that would take me back to my life as it was before. I couldn't sleep. I couldn't think. I had panic attacks. I developed anxiety so consuming that I couldn't be around people, much less work and function as a 'normal' person.

My perspective was altered. I was sick.

That trauma was my tipping point. PTSD, the complex, multiple trauma kind, set in. I fell into heavy daily use of marijuana to cope with all the symptoms and my life was irreversibly changed.

Looking back, I know that I have had similar, less debilitating episodes like this at other points in my life. Each one was worse than the last. This particular battle, my zero point, was beyond any coping mechanism I had.

I regressed, lashing out like a child. I followed the chaos of my head into a dark little rabbit hole of memories and lived them all over again. The truth is that the memories were always there, I had just lost my ability to push them aside and carry on.

It took a long time to get to this point and several secondary traumas. I have to admire the strength that held me together... and the denial. I had spent so much energy avoiding the truth, avoiding the acknowledgement of what was going on inside my head, and ignoring the effect that it had on me. When my reserve was gone, it was completely gone. I had no strength left. There was no energy remaining to keep the chaos under control. I collapsed under the weight of it.

My father was an alcoholic and he sexually abused me. He was a bitter, selfish, manipulative person, with a temper that exploded at whoever was around that would take it. In public, he was charming and generous, as sociopaths can often be. He was deceptively intelligent, with a mind I actually admired, despite his other failings. Whatever he was, there was a time when I was his little girl and I loved him, but he hurt me more than anyone else in my life.

My earliest memory of sexual abuse by my father is at about three or four years old. The details of that experience are burned into my brain, along with many other experiences through the years. The abuse continued until I was 16 and left my his house for good.

My father was the principal abuser, but there were others. I believe that what he did to me made me more vulnerable to the approaches of other men. For so many years, I had no understanding of what was really going on. My realization of the wrongness of it happened slowly; hurting more as I grew older and my awareness and understanding grew. It was a shame that became harder and harder to hide from myself.

My mother divorced him and they each remarried when I was nine. We lived in poverty most of the time, moving far too often between trailer parks and housing projects, chased away by debts or lured by a job to replace the last one that was lost.

There was no stable parenting in my life, the chaos of shuffling back-and-forth between my parents meant that much of what I needed as a child was neglected. I missed out on proper parenting and always felt I had missed out on love.

With all of the chaos, I went to 27 schools in eight states through high school. Being the new kid all the time left me vulnerable to bullying; reinforcing a sense of isolation that still keeps me somewhat distant from people.

Beyond this, there were other traumas. I had an accident when I was 11 with a concussion and facial injuries, which made me feel disfigured and ashamed and neglected even more. When I was 13, we lost my youngest brother to drowning – another case of outrageous neglect. He was only three years old.

Everything turned upside down after that. I started using marijuana. It helped me mask a lot of the emotions and deal with my situation and remained a part of my life from then on, until I had my children.

My first son was born when I was 18. My second came when I was 20, the same year as my divorce. Even though no-one really showed they believed in me, I knew I was capable of being a good mother. I pushed myself to make a good life for my children, to be a good parent, to somehow get beyond the addictions and poverty that had been such an issue for me. I found real happiness.

Life was more than just struggling, it was fun! My catch phrase in my 20's was "Just watch me!" I had a chip on my shoulder to prove myself. I worked two jobs when I needed the money. I did night classes, exemption testing, internships, TV classes, whatever I could do to improve my credentials... all the while supporting my little family. Somehow I balanced it all.

I started my first business when I was 25. I took my last paycheck from the CPA firm I was working for and started a consulting assignment with an Information Technology company. I was young and often passed over for formal roles, but I always had a good paycheck from then on.

I moved my family to Australia at 30. Not bad for a kid from the trailer park with no degree. I started my best venture, a management consulting company, when I was 33. I went on to live in three more countries and travelled all over the world.

Then I got sick and everything came crashing down.

A surgical mistake in 2003 resulted in secondary trauma that triggered Complex Post Traumatic Stress Disorder. I found myself in Intensive Care, numb to what was really going on, doped up on morphine and falling in upon myself. As I struggled to cope with the effects of that trauma, I couldn't push aside the thoughts and memories of my childhood. I couldn't silence my inner critic and couldn't handle the emotions that took over my life from there.

I took whatever prescriptions I was given and self-medicated with marijuana just so I could get through my days. I became numb. I tried to cope, but that became increasingly difficult as my anxieties worsened and my depression deepened.

Five years later, everything was unraveling. I was in a full-blown depressive episode, lying in bed and slowly starving myself to death. I had given up on living. My symptoms compounded, feeding a cycle of stress, metabolic dysfunction and mental unwellness until I simply couldn't function in the real world anymore.

The part of me that had strength was gone. All that was left was the dysfunctional little child I once was. I mourned myself. It was a death within a life. All I was left with was the shell of something I once was and I had no idea how to fill it with anything meaningful again.

When I became ill with CPTSD, it took me quite some time to understand that what was dealing with was an illness. I didn't have any real understanding of psychology... or psychobiology. I thought my emotions were character flaws and that my mixed-up comprehension was a short-circuit in my brain, or something like that.

The diagnosis of mental illness was confronting. I felt like I was being punished for being a bad person. I thought I was doomed. I hated that I was suddenly crazy... or maybe I was always crazy and now everyone would know it. I labeled myself with the same social stigma that keeps true compassion out of mental illness care. I fostered my own sense of shame.

It took time, but the more I learned about CPTSD, the more I understood that attaching shame to any condition makes it nearly impossible to find the hope needed to fight it. I had to work on my perspective in order to recover.

I learned that my condition is a natural human response to abnormal conditions of prolonged stress and recurrent trauma. In every person, trauma invokes response. This is a natural process. Stress also invokes response. Recurrent trauma and chronic stress turn these responses into a pattern of conditioned functioning that can either place a person on continual high-alert or routinely suppress cognitive awareness. Childhood traumas and stress cause even deeper issues, both biologically and psychologically... problems that can compound throughout a lifetime and eventually exhaust a person's ability to cope.

I found that everything I learned helped me to ultimately build a lasting foundation for my recovery. Understanding what I can about human psychobiology has enabled me to let go of a lot of the shame, blame and hopelessness of this condition. Now, I feel empowered in every small action I take toward healing myself.

Complex PTSD has certainly changed the course my life. Deciding to give my recovery priority meant that I had to give up my career. I thought I lost a valuable career because of my mental illness. I felt robbed of a meaningful and successful life by the man who allowed this, who caused all this and made me vulnerable to others who would exploit and abuse me. Decades after leaving my father's house, what he did to me was once again destroying my life.

On the early parts of this journey, I confronted so much loss. I was angry about everything, the loss of my prosperity, the loss of my health, the loss of my joy...

That has all faded as I've drawn perspective. For one, the career did not fit with my personal beliefs any longer. The more I discovered, the more I realized that I was fortunate to leave that work behind. Becoming more aware of the preciousness of life and the human experience has led me to a dramatically changed perspective of myself and others, a much healthier one that I have ever had.

I had no idea where it would lead me.

As I worked through my process, I wanted to understand why the problems I had as a kid were still affecting me. In the past, I had been told to just get over it, that it was all in the past and it shouldn't matter anymore. But I just didn't, I just couldn't get over it. It was impacting my life every single day. It was impacting the relationships I had, or tried to have. It was impacting everything. I couldn't trust, I couldn't sleep and I couldn't stand to be alone. I was scared and anxious more than I ever let on. I couldn't show weakness or sadness or anger because those were things that people could use against me.

But I knew. I knew that what was going on in my head had everything to do with the old traumas... as much as it did with the new ones. It was a pattern, one I was reliving every day. I was stuck and it was hurting me. The pain just got deeper and for a long while I felt lost... just like I did sometimes when I was a child.

I had tried getting to some understanding with my father. I had given him the opportunity to get it out and on the table. I wanted to understand his side of it. I wanted to understand what would make a father see his child like that. I wanted to know why.

But the answers I needed wouldn't come from him directly. In fact, what I was really looking for in all of this was an understanding of what I had done wrong, why it had happened to me.

I wanted to know what was wrong with me… more than I wanted to know what had been wrong about me that he would want to do those things to me.

I stopped all my medications, except for marijuana. I let the process behind my C-PTSD happen naturally and used it to finally heal those old wounds. I journalled and inventoried and narrated my history and my dreams for myself. I looked at my life more forgivingly and found acceptance. What I have gained from this process is beyond what I expected. I expected to find a place for my memories and lay them to rest, which has been the case so far. What I didn't expect was to grow so well beyond them, to find a gratitude for the whole of my life and to find a special love for myself as a result.

I have come a far way from being a victim to being a survivor… to something for which I have no term that fits. I am more than a survivor; I am more complete that I have ever been as a person. I feel more love, appreciation and gratitude for my life than I may ever have had without the experiences, traumatic as they may have been. Through this process, I have defined and reinforced values and life lessons I missed in my early development, which have impacted my view of myself and others.

Everything in my life has changed a great deal and it has taken time to accept those changes. I cannot go back to the way I used to live. I can't work in the high pressure environment that gave me so many opportunities and so much satisfaction before. But, focusing on what I can't do hasn't really led me to anything more than depression. I've had to move beyond this and find meaning in what I have and what I can still do.

I will continue to deal with chronic health issues. I have had to accept that I will likely need the support of marijuana for the rest of my life. For me, it is a better option than any pharmaceutical treatment, and I no longer find this as a point of shame either.

I have also opted for a single life, a simple domesticity without a partner. Too many of my triggers are rooted in home life and interpersonal conflict. I would love to say that I have moved past them all, but some conditioning is too deeply set. I am happy getting to know and love myself for probably the first time in my life.

When I started on this journey, I couldn't fathom the deep changes that I needed to go through or that the result would ultimately be so peaceful... so expansive. Nor did I realize that I wouldn't find the glowing full recovery that I had hoped for. I am in remission, but I know that I have to continually manage my stress and try to minimize triggers. I also have to maintain my health and avoid anything that might complicate my symptoms. This means managing my blood sugar, keeping up with my fitness and avoiding toxins as much as possible.

I thought about delaying this book a bit longer, hoping that I would have something miraculous to share, but the truth is that CPTSD has changed my life and the way I live. It just took some time, effort and understanding to appreciate those changes and accept them. I am happy to say that I feel that I've tackled the most challenging part of the process.

# References

1. Scared Sick: The Role of Childhood Trauma in Adult Disease, R Karr-Morse, http://books.google.com/books?hl=en&lr=&id=L6aqlTtCoQcC&oi=fnd&pg=PR9&dq=Scared+Sick:+The+Role+of+Childhood+Trauma+in+Adult+Disease&ots=g-zPNdlMn2&sig=K9auUCp95IsY2844advz_58WUV0#v=onepage&q=Scared%20Sick%3A%20The%20Role%20of%20Childhood%20Trauma%20in%20Adult%20Disease&f=false
2. What's the Real Diagnosis?, P Epstein, http://ndnr.com/mindbody/childhood-trauma-and-adult-disease/
3. Relationship of Childhood Abuse and Household Dysfunction to Many of the Leading Causes of Death in Adults: The Adverse Childhood Experiences (ACE) Study, V Felitti, R Anda, D Nordenberg, D Williamson, A Spitz, V Edwards, M Koss, J Marks, American Journal of Preventative Medicine, http://www.ajpmonline.org/article/S0749-3797(98)00017-8/abstract
4. The 4Fs: A Trauma Typology in Complex PTSD, P Walker, http://www.pete-walker.com/fourFs_TraumaTypologyComplexPTSD.htm
5. Developmental trauma disorder: Towards a rational diagnosis for children with complex trauma histories, B van der Kolk, http://www.traumacenter.org/products/pdf_files/preprint_dev_trauma_disorder.pdf
6. Blockade of GABA(A) receptors in the paraventricular nucleus of the hypothalamus attenuates voluntary ethanol intake and activates the hypothalamic-pituitary-adrenocortical axis, Li J, Bian W, Dave V, Ye JH, http://www.ncbi.nlm.nih.gov/pubmed/21762292
7. Localization of glutamatergic/aspartatergic neurons projecting to the hypothalamic paraventricular nucleus studied by retrograde transport of [3H]D-aspartate autoradiography, Csáki A, Kocsis K, Halász B, Kiss J, http://www.ncbi.nlm.nih.gov/pubmed/11113313
8. Pituitary-Adrenal and Autonomic Responses to Stress in Women After Sexual and Physical Abuse in Childhood, C Heim, DJ Newport, S Heit, Y Graham, M Wilcox, R Bonsall, A Miller, C Nemeroff, Journal of American Medicine, http://jama.jamanetwork.com/article.aspx?articleid=192947
9. Eating Disorder, Wikipedia, http://en.wikipedia.org/wiki/Eating_disorder
10. Diagnostic and Statistical Manual of Mental Disorder (DSM-5), American Psychiatric Association, http://www.psychiatry.org/practice/dsm/dsm-iv-tr

11. Obsessive-Compulsive Disorder, Wikipedia, http://en.wikipedia.org/wiki/Ocd
12. The Deliberate Self-Harm Syndrome, EM Pattison, J Kahan, http://ajp.psychiatryonline.org/article.aspx?articleID=160799
13. Childhood Trauma and Chronic Illness in Adulthood: Mental Health and Socioeconomic Status as Explanatory Factors and Buffers, S Mock, S Arai, Frontiers in Psychology, http://www.ncbi.nlm.nih.gov/pmc/articles/PMC3153850/
14. Endocannabinoid System, Wikipedia, http://en.wikipedia.org/wiki/Endocannabinoid_system
15. PTSD contributes to teen and young adult cannabis use disorders, J Cornelius, L Kirisci, M Reynolds, D Clark, J Hayes, R Tarter, http://www.sciencedirect.com/science/article/pii/S0306460309002366
16. The Myth of Resilient Children, Psychology Today, by Jessica Grogan, Ph.D., originally published in Encountering America. http://www.psychologytoday.com/blog/encountering-america/201302/the-myth-resilient-children
17. The Posttraumatic Growth Inventory: Measuring the Positive Legacy of Trauma, Journal of Traumatic Stress, Vol. 9, No. 3, 1996, by R. Tedeschi and L Calhoun, http://66.199.228.237/boundary/Childhood_trauma_and_PTSD/PosttraumaticGrowthInventory.pdf
18. Accumulated Childhood Trauma and Symptom Complexity, Journal of Traumatic Stress, Vol. 21, No. 2, 2008, J Briere, S Kaltman, B Green, http://www.johnbriere.com/JTS%20sx%20complexity.pdf
19. Childhood Trauma Leaves Its Mark on the Brain, Translational Psychiatry, 2013, C Sandi et al, ScienceBlog, http://scienceblog.com/59120/childhood-trauma-leaves-its-mark-on-the-brain/#WQ7sC77HGLBYAEWo.99
20. Post-Traumatic Stress Disorder – What Happens in the Brain?, Journal of the Washington Academy of Sciences, S Howard, M Crandall, http://www.washacadsci.org/Journal/Journalarticles/V.93-3-Post%20Traumatic%20Stress%20Disorder.%20Sethanne%20Howard%20and%20Mark%20CrandallI.pdf
21. PTSD: A Disease of Body and Mind, Hypoglycemic Health Association, J Plesman, http://www.hypoglycemia.asn.au/2011/post-traumatic-stress-disorder-ptsd-a-disease-of-body-and-mind/
22. Countering Brain Chemical Could Prevent Suicides, Michigan State University, A McGlashen, L Brundin, http://msutoday.msu.edu/news/2012/countering-brain-chemical-could-prevent-suicides/
23. Endocrine Disruptors, GreenFacts, http://www.greenfacts.org/en/endocrine-disruptors/endocrine-disruptors.htm

24. Global Assessment of the State-of-the-Science of Endocrine Disruptors, World Health Organization, http://www.who.int/ipcs/publications/new_issues/endocrine_disruptors/en/
25. The Impacts of Endocrine Disruptors on Wildlife, People and Their Environments, The Weybridge+15 Report, European Environment Agency, http://www.eea.europa.eu/publications/the-impacts-of-endocrine-disrupters
26. Interview with Dr. Russell Blaylock on Devastating Health Effects of MSG, Aspartame and Excitotoxins, NaturalNews.com, M Adams, http://www.naturalnews.com/020550_excitotoxins_MSG.html
27. The Therapeutic Relationship as the Foundation for Treatment with Adult Survivors of Sexual Abuse, K Olio, W Cornell, http://kspope.com/memory/relationship.php
28. Touch, The Unspoken Language – Healing from Sexual Abuse (Part II), The Cerio Institute, D Cerio, http://www.thecerioinstitute.com/publications/touchpartii.html
29. The Sexual Healing Journey : A Guide for Survivors of Sexual Abuse, W Maltz, http://www.healthysex.com/page/the-sexual-healing-journey
30. Getting Back in Touch for Survivors of Abuse, Making Up Lost Ground, http://www.makinguplostground.com/readpost.asp?id=9
31. The Body Keeps the Score: Memory and the Evolving Psychobiology of Post-Traumatic Stress, Trauma Information Pages, 1994, B van der Kolk, http://homepage.psy.utexas.edu/homepage/class/psy394U/Bower/03%20Emot,%20Trauma,Mem/Body%20keeps%20the%20score.%20Kolk%20.pdf
32. Self-Imagination Can Enhance Memory in Healthy and Memory-Impaired Individuals, Clinical Psychological Science, M Grilli, E Glisky, http://scienceblog.com/57567/self-imagination-can-enhance-memory-in-healthy-and-memory-impaired-individuals/#rO1W4UwIPpt2hspX.99
33. Effective Treatment of Complex Post Traumatic Stress Disorder and Early Attachment Trauma, 2011, UST Research Online, E Murphrey, http://ir.stthomas.edu/cgi/viewcontent.cgi?article=1003&context=caps_gradpsych_docproj
34. The Family Dynamics of Severe Child Abuse, Psychology Today, D Allen, http://www.psychologytoday.com/blog/matter-personality/201111/the-family-dynamics-severe-child-abuse
35. Inscribed Bodies: Health Impact of Childhood Sexual Abuse, A Kirkengen, http://books.google.com/books?hl=en&lr=&id=KDg9NTGHXrYC&oi=fnd&pg=PA1&dq=endometriosis+and+sexual+abuse+link&ots=zIPXyihis-&sig=2llFH-QW6bBaOA_D1ycwDKtv0AQ#v=onepage&q&f=false
36. The Health Impacts on Adult Women of Childhood Sexual Violence before the Age of Twelve Years, Minnesota Center Against Violence and Abuse, K

Hughes et al, http://www.mincava.umn.edu/documents/report/report.html
37. The Science of Resilience, Huffington Post Science Blog, S Southwick, http://www.huffingtonpost.com/steven-m-southwick/trauma-resilience_b_1881666.html?utm_hp_ref=science
38. From Child Sexual Abuse to Adult Sexual Risk: Trauma, Revictimization and Intervention, by Linda Keonig et al, http://www.apa.org/pubs/books/4317016.aspx
39. Sexuality Issues for Adult Survivors of Incest and Child Sexual Abuse, Research & Advocacy Digest, 2001, W Maltz, http://www.wcsap.org/sites/www.wcsap.org/files/uploads/documents/sexuality2001.pdf
40. Adult Manifestations of Childhood Sexual Abuse, Los Angeles Public Health Department, http://publichealth.lacounty.gov/wwwfiles/ph/media/media/TPH-409.pdf
41. Hyposexuality and Hypersexuality Secondary to Childhood Trauma, M Schwartz, Lori Galperin, http://www.castlewoodtc.com/wp-content/uploads/2011/07/hyposexuality-and-hypersexuality-secondary-to-childhood-trauma.pdf
42. Adult Sexual Health and Childhood Sexual Abuse, ReporterNews, P Irby, http://www.reporternews.com/news/2009/may/06/effects-abuse-part-5/
43. Substance Use, Childhood Traumatic Experience and Post-Traumatic Stress Disorder in an Urban Civilian Population, Depress Anxiety, 2010, L Khoury et al, http://www.ncbi.nlm.nih.gov/pmc/articles/PMC3051362/
44. How Childhood Trauma Creates Life-Long Adult Addicts, The Fix, http://www.thefix.com/content/trauma-and-addiction9180
45. The Rebel Doctor, The Fix, http://www.thefix.com/content/dr-gabor-mate-on-addiction-10076?page=1
46. Recognizing Complex Trauma, Psychology Today, 2012, L Firestone, www.psychologytoday.com/blog/compassion-matters/201207/recognizing-complex-trauma
47. Childhood Adversity Increases Risk for Depression and Chronic Inflammation, ScienceBlog, http://scienceblog.com/55340/childhood-adversity-increases-risk-for-depression-and-chronic-inflammation/
48. Abnormal Cortisol Levels, Depression, Anxiety, and PTSD Are Signs of Long-Term Abuse and Psychological Trauma, Emedia Health, http://emediahealth.com/2011/07/27/abnormal-cortisol-levels-depression-anxiety-and-ptsd-are-signs-of-long-term-abuse-and-psychological-trauma/
49. The Impact of Early Adversity on Children's Development, Center on the Developing Child at Harvard University, http://developingchild.harvard.edu/index.php/download_file/-/view/65/

50. Addictions and Trauma Recovery, International Society for the Study of Dissociation, 2000, J Fisher, http://janinafisher.com/pdfs/addictions.pdf
51. Abuse-Focused Therapy for Adult Survivors of Child Sexual Abuse: A Review of the Literature, Injury Prevention Research Centre, 2000, K McGregor, www.google.com/url?sa=t&rct=j&q=&esrc=s&source=web&cd=2&cad=rja&ved=0CEIQFjAB&url=http%3A%2F%2Fwww.fmhs.auckland.ac.nz%2Fsoph%2Fcentres%2Fipic%2F_docs%2Fcr51.pdf&ei=a0omUbaePJSI9ATc2IDgAw&usg=AFQjCNGMX8_31hQMqst-y0zLxaDltWS8Hw&sig2=Z6TlQt1lACn3Okpmt5j7QA&bvm=bv.42661473,d.eWU
52. Emotional Flashback Management in the Treatment of Complex PTSD, Psychotherapy.net, P Walker, http://www.psychotherapy.net/article/complex-ptsd
53. Post-Traumatic Stress Disorder for Dummies, M Goulston, http://www.wiley.com/WileyCDA/WileyTitle/productCd-0470049227,descCd-tableOfContents.html
54. What Part of the Brain Does PTSD Affect? EHow.com, L Stannard, http://www.ehow.com/facts_5132904_part-brain-ptsd-effect.html
55. PTSD Adrenal Symptoms, LiveStrong, A Walding, http://www.livestrong.com/article/98396-ptsd-adrenal-symptoms/
56. Post Traumatic Growth Inventory: Measuring the Positive Legacy of Trauma, Journal of Traumatic Stress, Vol. 9, No. 3, 1996, R Tedeschi, L Calhoun,http://66.199.228.237/boundary/Childhood_trauma_and_PTSD/PosttraumaticGrowthInventory.pdf
57. Violence Puts Wear and Tear on Kids' DNA, EurekAlert, K Morgan, http://www.eurekalert.org/pub_releases/2012-04/du-vpw041812.php
58. Mildly Stressful Situations Can Affect Our Perceptions in the Same Way As Life-Threatening Ones, Health and Medical News, http://jflahiff.wordpress.com/2012/06/18/mildly-stressful-situations-can-affect-our-perceptions-in-the-same-way-as-life-threatening-ones/
59. Ariz. Vets: Allow Medical Marijuana for PTSD, The Arizona Republic, Y Sanchez, http://mindmejournal.wordpress.com/2012/06/05/airforcetimes-com-article-medical-marijuana-helps-vets-with-ptsd/
60. Medical Marijuana Use and Mental Disorders, weedhubca, http://weedhubca.wordpress.com/2012/06/13/medical-marijuana-use-and-mental-disorder/
61. Six Ways to Recovery From Complex Trauma or Complex PTSD, counselorssoapbox, http://counselorssoapbox.com/2012/06/09/6-ways-to-recover-from-complex-trauma-or-complex-ptsd/

62. Do I Have PTSD?, Dr. Kathleen Young: Treating Trauma, K Young, http://drkathleenyoung.wordpress.com/2012/06/08/do-i-have-ptsd/
63. Embattled Childhood: The Real "T" in PTSD, Huffington Post Health Blog, W Herbert, http://www.huffingtonpost.com/wray-herbert/embattled-childhood-the-r_b_1596729.html?utm_hp_ref=health-news&ir=Health%20News
64. Child Abuse Accommodation Syndrome, Child Abuse and Neglect, Vol. 7, 1983, R Summit, http://www.google.com/url?sa=t&rct=j&q=&esrc=s&source=web&cd=3&ved=0CEwQFjAC&url=http%3A%2F%2Fwww.ou.edu%2Fcwtraining%2Fassets%2Fpdf%2Fhandouts%2F1012%2FThe%2520Child%2520Sexual%2520Abuse%2520Accommodation%2520Syndrome.doc&ei=Y1kmUbmBL5L08ASj94CoAg&usg=AFQjCNG8-_G6ugaZxmLGu6xRL3AleTpNPg&sig2=jyoYlrTCc98KsECzOjrNRA&bvm=bv.42661473,d.eWU&cad=rja
65. Childhood Trauma and Psychosis, Dialogues Clin Neurosci, 2011, I Shafer, H Fisher, http://www.ncbi.nlm.nih.gov/pmc/articles/PMC3182006/
66. A developmental approach to complex PTSD: Childhood and adult cumulative trauma as predictors of symptom complexity, Journal f Traumatic Stress, International Society for Traumatic Stress Studies, 2009, M. Cloitre et al, http://onlinelibrary.wiley.com/doi/10.1002/jts.20444/abstract;jsessionid=FFD324E8B674F4610B759DE7BA2BD61B.f02t03?deniedAccessCustomisedMessage=&userIsAuthenticated=false
67. Endocannabinoid System Participates in Neuroendocrine Control of Homeostasis; De Laurentiis, Fernández Solari, Mohn, Zorrilla Zubilete,Rettori; Centro de Estudios Farmacológicos y Botánicos, CEFYBO-CONICET-UBA, Facultad de Medicina, Universidad de Buenos Aires, Buenos Aires , Argentina; http://www.odon.uba.ar/uacad/fisiologia/docs/nuevos/endocannabinoid.pdf

12517741R00033

Printed in Great Britain
by Amazon.co.uk, Ltd.,
Marston Gate.